The General Theory of Unemployment

The General Theory of Unemployment

The fatal legacy of Adam
Smith and the rehabilitation
of John Maynard Keynes

Vernon Routley

Typeset by BookPOD

Disclaimer
The material in this book is general comment only and neither
purports nor intends to be specific advice related to any particular
reader. It does not represent professional advice and should not be
relied on as the basis for any decision or action on any matter that
it covers. To the maximum extent permitted by law, the author and
publisher disclaim all responsibility and liability to any person or
entity, whether a purchaser or not, in respect to anything and of
the consequences of anything done by any such person in reliance,
whether in whole or in part, upon the whole or any part of the
contents of this publication.

ISBN: 978-0-6483296-0-2 (pbk)
eISBN: 978-1-925457-81-0 (e-book)

CONTENTS

PREFACE

Since the end of World War II, the economics profession has failed the community through its inability to distinguish clearly between the ordered stable microeconomic world of Adam Smith and the indeterminate unstable macroeconomic world of John Maynard Keynes and to simply treat the latter as an adjunct or extension of the former.

Microeconomics is a readily understandable concept. It embraces the myriad transactions to buy and sell goods and services which most individuals are, more or less continually, undertaking.

Macroeconomics is a less immediately obvious concept. It encompasses the vast range of activities, social and political as well as economic, wherewith any community – from a roving tribe of hunter-gatherers to a modern nation state – uses the resources at its disposal to achieve its preferred objectives. Until John Maynard Keynes arrived on the scene, macroeconomics did not exist as a separate concept in the economic lexicon. There is no evidence within the voluminous writings of Adam Smith which would suggest that he was even aware of its existence.

In the microeconomic world of Adam Smith, the market is the dominant force. The continuing interaction of demand, supply and price provides an environment wherein individuals motivated purely by self-interest are led to co-operate in ways which result in an increased volume of goods and services becoming available to the community. At the same time the market ensures there will be no permanently idle resources: in the case of the labour force there will be no long-term unemployment as workers respond to a fall in the demand for their services by moving to other areas, industries or occupations or by accepting lower wages.

In the macroeconomic world of John Maynard Keynes, the market plays no direct role at all. The total supply of labour and the total demand for it can be identified but there is no overall price which equilibrates the two. Instead there are a multitude of individual prices, each arising from an equal number of individual contracts for the purchase and sale of human services. Any equilibration of total supply and total demand, which intuition alone would suggest is always tending to occur, does so without any obvious guiding influence. In such an unstructured situation there is no reason why varying levels of unemployment should not be a normal feature of the economic and social environment.

As for the appropriate relationship between micro- and macroeconomics, it should be seen as one of coexistence: two separate phenomena operating independently whenever and wherever the community engages in economic activity.

In the microeconomic world of Adam Smith unemployment is a purely economic problem caused by any of a number of extraneous factors interfering with the normal operation of market forces.

In the macroeconomic world of John Maynard Keynes, unemployment is also a social problem, affecting mainly those sections of the working age population whose employability ratings are in the lower end of the range, mostly unskilled and semi-skilled workers.

CHAPTER 1

The background

'The other day upon the stair,
I met a man who wasn't there.
He wasn't there again today.
I wish that man would go away.'

In any exchange economy capital, labour and resources are combined in varying ways to satisfy the community demand for goods and services. Depending on the size of the economy this can involve millions, even trillions of individual decisions to buy or sell – to demand or supply labour. However there is no reason why, for any given time and place, the overall demand for labour will equate with the total number of individuals offering their services. Theoretically this might lead to a state of overfull employment with inflationary consequences arising from wage cost pressures in the labour market. The economic history of the last three centuries, however, endorses the conclusion reached by John Maynard Keynes in 1936: 'That evidence indicates that full, or even approximately full, employment is of rare and short-lived occurrence.'[1]

Unemployment was not actually recognized as an independent social phenomenon until the nineteenth century, by which time the adverse consequences of the economic changes being wrought by the Industrial Revolution were becoming more and more apparent.

Early economic writers were optimists, understandably so since they were living in economies expanding as a result of the inflationary forces unleashed by the flood of gold and silver spreading across Europe following the Spanish conquest of central and South America, and, as is usually the case with changes, it was the middle and upper classes who were the main beneficiaries.

Among the most optimistic of the early economic writers was Adam Smith who in 1776 published his *Inquiry into the Nature and Causes of the Wealth of Nations* – now universally abbreviated to *The Wealth of Nations*, and now also recognized as one of the most influential books ever published in the English language.

In publishing *The Wealth of Nations*, Adam Smith changed the focus of public debate from macroeconomics to microeconomics. Prior to Adam Smith the approach to economic analysis had been holistic, viewing the

---

1 John Maynard Keynes, *The General Theory of Employment, Interest and Money.* London: Macmillan, 1951.

entire economy as a single entity, with the government at the centre of affairs, directing or sponsoring activities which could be seen as promoting the further increase of national wealth. Adam Smith's approach to economic affairs was essentially parochial, concentrating on individual areas, industries or occupations with the government playing a purely supporting role in ensuring a secure economic environment. Within such an environment, individuals pursuing enlightened self-interest would combine with others in various ways to increase the overall volume of goods and services available to the community.

The economic writers who preceded Adam Smith had a basically negative attitude to unemployment. Insofar as it was actually recognized, it was lumped together with poverty, sickness, disease and crime as blemishes on an otherwise optimistic scenario of steadily increasing economic progress. As individuals, the unemployed were viewed unsympathetically. Under the Poor Law systems which had operated in Great Britain from Elizabethan times, no distinction was made between vagrants and the jobless. Both were simply categorized as 'sturdy beggars' to be punished and moved on.

Adam Smith with his background as a moral philosopher was broadly sympathetic to the unemployed as individuals but there was no place in his economic lexicon for unemployment as a separately identifiable economic phenomenon. In his microeconomic world of individual occupations, industries and areas, unemployment simply could not occur. The operations of the market – the interaction of demand, supply and prices – ensured that whenever the demand for labour fell workers would respond either by reducing the asking price for their services or moving elsewhere to other areas, industries or occupations.

Even as Adam Smith was writing however, attractive theory was being undermined by unattractive reality. The British textile industry was being transformed as machines progressively replaced individual handcraft operators. Unable to compete on price, these operators – the first victims of the Industrial Revolution – now faced a future of unemployment and poverty.

Despite living in the midst of such social disruption Adam Smith appears to have been unaware of it. Certainly there is no mention of it in his book. For that matter there is no direct reference to unemployment either. As George Orwell might have said, for Adam Smith unemployment was simply a 'non-fact'.

A generation after Adam Smith, the French economist Jean-Baptiste Say published his *Treatise on Political Economy*. A self-declared disciple of Adam Smith, he advanced the proposition that, for the economy as a whole, supply created its own demand; individuals produced goods or services, sold them to others, then used the income so derived to purchase goods or services offered by others. This seductive half-truth offered no explanation of how the matching process actually operated. Workers were ready enough to offer their services but if employers were not interested, workers would have no income and therefore no demand for the goods and services offered by others. As Keynes was to point out more than a century later, Say's Law, as this proposition came to be referred to, was only valid when an economy was already operating at the level of full employment.

Say's Law was not really a law at all. It did not identify any particular course of action. It was no more than a description of a highly desirable state of economic affairs.

Say certainly shifted the focus of economic discussions away from the microeconomic approach of Adam Smith towards the macroeconomic approach of his predecessors. No more than Adam Smith, however, did Say regard unemployment as a specific, economic concept requiring separate analysis within the corpus of economic debate. And so the unwelcome gentleman on the nursery stairs remained ensconced there!

CHAPTER 2

Economic theory
and political reality

In the western world, the first fifteen years of the nineteenth century were dominated by the attempts of Napoleon Bonaparte to achieve the hegemony of France in Europe and the efforts of most of the other countries to prevent him from doing so. This continuing struggle provided an ongoing economic stimulus offering secure, and mostly paid, employment to several million men, including those most vulnerable to unemployment. And behind the combatants thousands of enterprises were providing not only arms and other military equipment, but also the wide range of paraphernalia required to maintain the fighting capacity of any army.

Then, on 16 June 1815, everything changed abruptly. Defeated at Waterloo, Napoleon disappeared into permanent exile on St Helena. And with Napoleon also went the economic stimulus he had unwittingly provided. Military orders from governments quickly dried up and soldiers were steadily demobilized. The unemployment that followed could no longer be completely ignored in the way Smith and Say had been able to do.

Faced with this new reality, economic theorists, disciples of Smith and Say, responded in two different ways. First, while affirming the role of the market in establishing equilibrium between buyers and sellers, they were prepared to admit that it did not always operate in the smooth, direct fashion theory assumed. Non-economic factors intervened; wars, natural disasters and human psychology as exhibited in the failure of suppliers of goods and services to adjust readily to changes in the demand for them. This seemed to be particularly so in the case of workers, who were usually both reluctant to accept lower wages or to move elsewhere. From this observation it was a small step to the belief that workers were, at least partly, responsible for their own unemployment. This plausible half-truth naturally appealed to employers – domestic, commercial and industrial alike – and since this group represented the dominant political force in the nineteenth century, the belief soon became part of the conventional economic wisdom.

The second approach of the economic theorists to increased unemployment was to follow the example of Smith and Say and minimize the significance of unemployment in the overall economic environment. Instead they turned their attention to how the output of goods and services could be increased and to how that output came to be distributed among the three main factors of production – land, labour and capital – in the form of rents, wages and profits. Thus John Stuart Mill, the most important economic writer in the second half of the nineteenth century, makes no direct references to unemployment anywhere in his *Principles of Political Economy*, first published in 1848. Similarly, Alfred Marshall, doyen of academic economists, was able to overlook unemployment entirely in his *Principles of Economics*, first published in 1890.

The political realists, led by the Frenchman, J. C. L. de Sismondi, and the Englishman, J. R. Malthus, saw unemployment as an ongoing economic problem warranting serious attention from the government. Both published economic texts: Sismondi, *New Principles of Political Economy* in 1819 and Malthus, *Principles of Political Economy* in 1820.

Both Sismondi and Malthus adopted the macroeconomic approach to the world that prevailed prior to the arrival of Adam Smith. Both viewed unemployment as part of a wider problem of 'general gluts'. This was a term borrowed from agriculture where occasional bountiful seasons produced a supply of some foods beyond the immediate demand for them. Unfortunately neither of the two men could offer a plausible explanation for such oversupply and particularly for any oversupply of labour. They were in fact locked into Adam Smith's microeconomic world where labour supply was flexible whereas in their macroeconomic world labour supply was inflexible, simply being the existing working-age population that in the short term was essentially a fixed quantity.

For more than a century after Waterloo, unemployment and its causes were the subject of a continuing, if desultory, debate between the theorists and the pragmatists. Neither side, however, grasped the essential distinction between Adam Smith's microeconomic view of the world wherein market forces were always tending to equilibrium in individual areas, industries and occupations, and the macroeconomic world where the major factors of production, land (or resources), labour and capital, combine in a multiplicity of ways to satisfy the wants of consumers but do so without any overall guiding force and without any obvious certainty as to the ultimate outcome of their activities.

Yet despite the apparent anarchy that characterises economics at the macroeconomic level, and a continual if varying level of unemployment, western societies have still witnessed a remarkable level of economic growth over the period since Adam Smith published *The Wealth of Nations*. The benefits of such growth however have been skewed in favour of the great majority of individuals who have gainful employment or

enjoy an independent source of income. The remainder
– up to 10 per cent of the population – represents a
sort of economic underclass comprised mainly of the
unemployed, the underemployed and the intermittently
employed, who have much less to be thankful for. They
might be compared to servants gleaning the remains of a
banquet once the guests have left. Those guests passing
the nursery stairs on the way out would usually have
averted their eyes from the unwanted gentleman still
firmly ensconced thereon.

CHAPTER 3

The man who died too soon

Seen in the broad historical perspective, unemployment has always operated as something of a brake on economic progress, relatively light in periods of prosperity, rather heavier in periods of recession. The varying levels of unemployment also help to account for the irregularity which has usually characterised the upward trend in economic growth. Until the fourth decade of the twentieth century, however, unemployment had never threatened to seriously delay, let alone reverse, the process.

Thus in the third decade of the twentieth century – the 1920s – as the western world was recovering from the trauma of World War I there was no reason why most people should not be looking at the future with a justifiable degree of optimism. At the very end of the decade, the rosy glow suddenly began to fade. The stock market bubble of the later 1920s collapsed in October 1929, the exuberance generated by its expansion being replaced by feelings first of fear and then of pessimism. Consumers cut back on their spending wherever they could. Businesses decided to hold off on new investment, at least for the time being. Inevitably unemployment rose and kept on rising. Economic growth slowed to a halt and even began to reverse.

It was a bewildering situation. The familiar economic system which heretofore had generated a steady rise in living standards had now produced a situation of 'poverty in the midst of plenty'. Governments, baffled by this unexpected turn of events and subjected to a range of advice from various quarters, resorted to a series of ad hoc policies, some of which involved more public spending while others involved less, but none of which seemed to result in any significant reduction in unemployment.

Some observers even began to wonder if the capitalist economic system might not have run its course, particularly when compared to the apparent success of the Five Year Plans adopted by the Soviet Union where by all accounts no one was starving and unemployment was said to be negligible.

Then in 1936 after six years of economic depression, John Maynard Keynes published *The General Theory of Employment, Interest and Money* (hereafter abbreviated to *The General Theory*). The book was a direct challenge to the current conventional economic wisdom which still held the belief that a competitive, free-market economy had a normal tendency to full employment, despite abundant evidence to the contrary. Keynes on the other hand asserted that historical evidence, going back at least to the days of Adam Smith, showed that a competitive, free-market economy has a normal tendency to exhibit a significant and continuing level of unemployment. In other words, where conventional economic wisdom continued to regard unemployment as an unfortunate aberration in an otherwise effectively operating system, Keynes now viewed it as a normal feature of a freely operating capitalist economy.

At this point the focus of the analysis moved from the micro world of Adam Smith, wherein demand, supply and price interacted within individual sectors of the economy to promote equilibrium, to the macro world of the whole economy viewed as a single entity in much the same way as the predecessors of Adam Smith had usually done.

In the macroeconomic context, any oversupply of labour simply reflected an oversupply of the goods and services labour was employed to produce. Keynes was now back to the problem of 'gluts' with which Sismondi and Malthus had wrestled unsuccessfully. Unlike them, however, Keynes had freed himself from the straightjacket of microeconomics with which Adam Smith had surrounded any economic debate. He was thus able to investigate the issue of unemployment on the basis of first principles.

The starting point for Keynes was the recognition that in a capitalist economy, the total output of goods and services produced by the community always seemed to be somewhat greater than the overall demand of the community for them. Analysing overall demand, he identified two separate components: consumption demand and investment demand.

Consumption demand arises from income spent by individuals on the purchase of goods and services for their own personal requirements. Investment demand arises from income spent by businesses and individuals on activities and projects which they anticipate will return a greater amount than the funds they originally have to outlay.

These two expenditure streams have a very different impact on economic activity. Consumption demand is relatively constant. Income spent on goods and services becomes income for the producers of such goods and services who then repeat the process in much the same fashion as J.-B. Say hypothesized at the beginning of the nineteenth century. Investment expenditure operates very differently. Its conversion into a demand for goods and services depends on individual assessments of the likely costs and expected benefits of any decisions to be made. These in turn depend not only on the economic, social and political conditions prevailing at any particular time and place but also on how favourable or unfavourable individuals perceive such conditions to be.

Seen from a macroeconomic perspective then, investment demand is simply a 'loose cannon' – indeterminate and unpredictable.

Certainly in no way could investment demand be guaranteed to absorb any output of goods and services left over from satisfying consumption demand. This being so, governments should always be ready to make up the shortfall with investment expenditure of their own.

At one and the same time, Keynes had not only provided a theoretical explanation for unemployment which was consistent with observable reality, but also offered a plausible method by which such unemployment might be eliminated. In the process he had also removed the disconnect between theory and reality which had bedevilled economic debate for more than a century while at the same time providing a firm theoretical foundation for the disconnected assortment of ad hoc measures whereby western governments were desperately trying to offset the worst effects of a seemingly endless depression.

Now for one of the great ironies of economic history! The regime which in the 1930s was most successfully following the Keynesian approach was Nazi Germany. In his pursuit of world domination, Adolf Hitler had provided the German economy with a massive economic stimulus by embarking on an open-ended rearmament program. Within three years of his accession to power the German economy was enjoying full employment and for the next four or five years the non-Jewish population of Germany was experiencing a level of economic prosperity unequalled anywhere in the contemporary world.

In response to the ever-increasing threat posed by Nazi Germany and, to a lesser extent, Imperial Japan, 'western' nations began in turn to rearm with a consequent reduction in their levels of unemployment. When Britain and France declared war on Germany in September 1939 they effectively mandated unemployment out of existence. Normal economic activity was subordinated to the overriding goal of defeating Germany. At the same time the United States was beginning to experience the direct and indirect benefits arising from its status of armed neutrality and by the time Japan launched its attack on Pearl Harbour, the American economy was also approaching full employment.

After 1943 as the threat of defeat receded and victory, although slow in coming, became ever more assured, attention began to turn towards the sort of world victory might bring and in particular to the intriguing possibility of peacetime full employment. Against this background, Sir William Beveridge in 1944 published his *Full Employment in a Free Society*, which in modern-day parlance might be described as 'Keynesian Economics for Dummies'.

Thus, by the time World War II ended, Keynes was at the height of his authority and prestige with 'western' governments responsive to whatever opinions he might care to express. By then however his health was failing. Nine months later he was dead, leaving to lesser mortals the task of wrestling with any issues which might emerge from the establishment of permanent peacetime full employment.

CHAPTER 4

Opening Pandora's box

At the time of his death it seemed that Keynes had bequeathed to the world a silver bullet capable of removing the problem of chronic unemployment which had plagued western economies for more than two centuries. With the benefit of hindsight it is now clear that what Keynes left the world was not so much a silver bullet as a Pandora's box. When opened this box revealed a number of unresolved questions. In particular:

i.   The need for a more precise definition of 'full employment' than simply 'the absence of involuntary unemployment'.[2]

ii. The extent of government intervention in the economy which would provide 'the controls necessary to ensure full employment while

---

2   John Maynard Keynes, *The General Theory of Employment, Interest and Money*, p. 15.

still maintaining a wide field for the exercise of private initiative'.[3]

iii. Whether 'full employment' should be seen as simply a means to an end – removing a serious impediment to economic growth – or an end in itself – empowering wage and salary earners by equalising bargaining power in the labour market.

Defining full employment

Full employment is a very attractive concept but it can, as Keynes realised,[4] always mutate into a less attractive phenomenon, that of overfull employment – a situation where inflationary wage cost pressures develop and adversely impact on the rest of the economy. In practice it can be difficult to determine at what level of labour demand such pressures begin to emerge, simply because the incidence of unemployment is not spread evenly across the labour force – quite the reverse in fact.

At any given level of economic activity unemployment will always be lowest for skilled or experienced workers (the premium labour force), and higher for unskilled and inexperienced workers (the non-premium labour force). In such a situation any efforts to reduce unem-

---

3   Keynes, p. 318.
4   Keynes, p. 30.

ployment in the non-premium labour force by raising the overall level of economic activity will increase the level of demand in the premium labour force and begin to generate inflationary wage cost pressures in that sector. The economy is faced with gridlock – reduce unemployment in the non-premium labour force and thereby increase inflationary wage cost pressures in the premium labour force, or limit inflationary pressures and increase unemployment in the non-premium labour force.

For the premium labour force, full employment is always a possibility but for the economy as a whole full employment is an unrealistic concept – a will-o'-the-wisp. The best that can be hoped for is some form of compromise which maximizes employment in the non-premium labour force while minimizing inflationary wage cost pressures in the premium labour force.

For this situation a new term such as 'optimum employment' would seem to be required. Such a term would distinguish the unrealistic concept of economy-wide full employment occurring at some specifically identifiable level of economic activity from the idea of an economic zone within which both price stability and full employment might be achieved independently, but not simultaneously. Given that such an economic zone could turn out to be fairly broad, the concept of optimizing would reflect the continuing adjustments such a situation would necessarily involve. It would also emphasize the importance of seeking to narrow such a zone whenever and wherever possible.

Government intervention in the economy

For Keynes, government intervention in the workings of the economy was never more than a least worst option. His views on the relative merits of government action versus individual initiative are entirely compatible with those of Adam Smith. They would have attracted ringing endorsements from Margaret Thatcher and Ronald Reagan had anyone brought his views to their attention. His paean to individualism on page 380 of *The General Theory* would gladden the hearts of true believers were they ever to get around to reading it.

Although *The General Theory* did not offer any specific advice on how a government should go about the task of establishing and maintaining full employment, it did introduce into the economic lexicon two new concepts: (i) the employment multiplier and (ii) the propensity to consume. These economic concepts can be of potentially enormous value to any government grappling with the endless tasks of maximizing the output of goods and services and of ensuring the appropriate distribution of that output among its citizens.

The employment multiplier

The employment multiplier identifies a fundamental feature of any exchange economy – the manner in which actions in one part of the economy will produce reactions in other parts. However, although being readily identifiable in any situation, its precise impact is unquantifiable after the fashion of ripples on a pond spreading out from the spot first hit by a stone – a phenomenon observable but unmeasurable. Keynes, however, was able to use the concept to assess the relative effectiveness of private and public investment in stimulating the economy and promoting employment.

Private investment is essentially a replacement exercise designed to produce a more effective or, at least, more popular means of meeting consumers' preferences. In the process however it will have adverse consequences on the incomes of those who were supplying goods and services under the previous arrangements. The net impact of private investment is thus significantly less than its initial or gross impact.

Public investment, particularly that designed to expand social infrastructure, has a minimal impact on the pre-existing labour force. Thus the gap between the gross and the net impact on the labour market is either non-existent or at worst only of minor significance.

Recognition of this distinction between public and private investment explains one of the initially puzzling sections of *The General Theory*, Book III, Chapter 10. In this part Keynes cites with approval pyramid building and the encouragement of gold mining and concludes with the whimsical suggestion that the government should bury old but usable bank notes in the bottom of abandoned coal mines and then proceed to auction off to the public the right to dig them up again. In each case the principal impact of these activities is the same – increasing the demand for labour in one sector of the economy in a way which will not involve a reduction in the demand for labour somewhere else.

Recognizing the distinction between the gross and net impact of an employment multiplier reduces any choice between public and private investment to questions of the costs involved and whether the former alternative can be financed without increasing public debt and thereby imposing on future taxpayers the burden of ongoing interest payments.

The propensity to consume

The propensity to consume measures the extent to which an individual spends his income as soon as it becomes available or retains some of it for future use. As an individual's income increases his spending on goods and services increases, but by less than the increase in income. At the bottom of the income hierarchy, the individual's propensity to consume will be 100 per cent and thereafter steadily decline as his income increases until, in the upper echelons of the income hierarchy, it falls to zero. At this stage the individual's propensity to consume becomes dormant and any further increases in income will simply be used in supplementing his existing financial assets.

In the case of individuals, a decline in the propensity to consume is an indication of increasingly favourable economic circumstances as the ability to put aside part of current income for future use increases the extent to which the individual is able to control his own economic destiny.

For governments, however, any decline in the propensity to consume for the population as a whole actually increases the problems of economic management. Insofar as consumption expenditure – the stable element of aggregate demand – declines, the government becomes more heavily dependent on the unstable element of aggregate demand, investment expenditure.

This in turn led to the disturbing conclusion, pointed out by Keynes in Chapter 10 of *The General Theory*, that the richer an economy becomes the more difficult it will be to manage, for it means a change in the composition of the aggregate demand which absorbs the ongoing output of goods and services, away from its stable component, consumption, and towards its unstable component, investment.

For this reason Keynes believed in supporting the role of consumption whenever and wherever possible and opposed anything which tended to reduce its significance. This view extended to the issues involved in funding government expenditure where there is always a choice between taxing consumption or taxing income.

Taxes on consumption, almost by definition, reduce the propensity to consume on the part of the community as a whole whereas taxes on income which mostly affect the more affluent sectors of the economy have far less effect. Most individuals in this group are already in the fortunate position of being able to choose how much of their income they will spend and how much of it they will save. While any increase in their tax will be resisted, its imposition is unlikely to change their pre-existing spending patterns.

Thus simply by introducing the concept of the propensity to consume into the economic lexicon Keynes was able to provide a valid economic argument for an ethical position – reducing the disparity in the distribution of national income – which he himself strongly supported.[5]

---

5 Keynes, p. 372.

Full employment: a means to an end or an end in itself

Since it began to emerge as a separately identifiable area of human behaviour some four centuries ago the central objective of economics has always been to increase the wealth of the community.

Throughout the period a wide range of propositions have emerged – some to disappear when the social and economic circumstances changed, others to persist indefinitely – but all of them revolved in some way around the central objective of increasing the material welfare of the community and the standard of living of its citizens or, in modern parlance, increased economic growth.

Initially the establishment of full employment would seem to be an obvious way of advancing this process, with previously unemployed labour resources now being utilized. In point of fact, however, the opposite situation tends to develop.

Experience during World War II and in the immediately following years of full or near full employment revealed that above a certain level of labour demand, new economic phenomena – in particular absenteeism and labour turnover – emerge and grow stronger the closer the economy comes to full employment. The result is a decline in labour productivity and an inevitable reduction in the rate of economic growth.

Seen in terms of social philosophy rather than economics any decline in labour productivity is simply a case of workers using the higher demand for their services and consequent increased bargaining power in the labour market to exercise a choice – a preference for less work rather than more income. Keynes, who considered himself a social philosopher as much as an economist (*The General Theory*, Chapter 24) strongly endorsed this view. Indeed in one of the flights of fancy with which he periodically regaled the cognoscenti, he looked forward to a situation in the twenty-first century where working time might be reduced to a mere three hours a day.[6]

Keynes was not opposed to economic growth as such. He simply regarded it as unimportant, or at least as less important than ensuring a situation where jobs were readily available to all those willing and able to work. For him, full employment was not simply a means to an end, but an end in itself. The situation Keynes was envisioning was also one where the bargaining power of employees matched that of employers.

---

6   John Maynard Keynes, *The Economic Possibilities for Our Grand-children*, Nation and Athenaeum, 11 & 18 October 1930.

In the modern parlance, Keynes was seeking – wittingly or unwittingly – to establish a level playing field in the labour market.

CHAPTER 5

The vision fades

In the generation following his death, Keynes's reputation plummeted – in 1946 an economic saviour, by the 1970s an economic scapegoat.

The process of decline was begun, unwittingly, by Keynes's disciples and supporters simply because they failed to take heed of his warning in *The General Theory* (p. 296) that full employment could have inflationary consequences via wage cost pressures developing in the labour market.

In the event, the inflationary consequences of a full employment policy turned out to be far greater than anyone might have imagined in 1936 when Keynes published *The General Theory* or in 1946 when he died.

To begin with, the obverse side of any full employment policy is to permanently underpin the price of the major factor in the production process of the economy – labour – and to ensure that any changes in that price can only be in an upward direction.

This economic distortion is magnified by the wide divergence within the labour force between those individuals whose services are in high demand and those who enjoy no such advantages and that, following from this divergence, the situation arises where, long before full employment is in sight for those at the lower end of the labour market, pressure for wages increases will be emerging among those in the top end.

At the same time, operating in the background, those sectors of the economy enjoying a degree of market power, monopolists or oligopolists, are able to exploit this advantage by increasing the price of their own particular product or service.

In 1936 such market power was mostly dormant in the face of universal buyer resistance to higher prices, but once economic activity begins to approach the full employment level monopolists and oligopolists are able to assert their power. This was particularly so in the case of trade unions.

Initially trade unions were perceived as worker protection organizations providing some form of counterweight – mostly psychological – to the dominance of employers in the buyer's market for labour characteristic of the economic conditions prevailing as the Industrial Revolution gathered strength.

In this 'protective' role, trade unions attracted widespread support not only among individual workers assembled in ever-increasing numbers of factories and mines, but also among wage earners generally and beyond them among those members of the middle classes not directly associated with commercial and industrial activities.

While the overall demand for labour was subdued, the overall power of trade unions was also fairly limited. But once the level of economic activity approached full employment the power of trade unions increased dramatically. They found buyer resistance to their demands far less. Employers were usually able to pass on increased labour costs by charging higher prices for their products, more often than not adding a little something extra along the way.

There was however a more basic reason for trade unions' vigorous pursuit of wage increases – self-preservation. In a very real sense full employment tends to make trade unions irrelevant. Once full employment has established a level playing field in the labour market, workers are no longer in need of protection. They can now negotiate on more or less equal terms with individual employers. In this environment trade unions must be able to demonstrate to the average worker that they can achieve more for them through continued group action than workers can achieve for themselves on their own initiative.

☣

Once the relevant institutional features embodied in any capitalist exchange economy are taken into account it seems inevitable, on purely theoretical grounds, that any attempts by any government to institute and maintain a state of full employment will have inescapably inflationary consequences.

And so it turned out. Within a few years, the continuing sellers' market for labour, reinforced by widespread monopoly and oligopoly in the labour and product markets, generated a rapid rise in wage rates and a consequently rapid increase in prices. This in turn led to governments imposing restraints on 'overheated' economies and, inevitably, the reappearance of unemployment.

For at least two decades after 1946 the economic history of western societies was dominated by an ongoing sequence of stop/go financial policies – first government action to absorb unemployment, then measures to reduce rising inflation levels followed in turn by further economic stimulus to reduce rising unemployment.

During the 1950s the simple objective of full employment was progressively modified by economists and politicians into a more complex one – Non-Inflationary Full Employment or N.I.F.E for short.

This 'rebranding' amounted to a de facto recognition of the fact that the pursuit of full employment involved some sort of choice between inflation on the one hand and unemployment on the other. Such recognition, however, did not lead to any significant policy initiatives and stop/go policies continued if only for lack of any apparent alternatives.

For almost a generation after World War II supporters of Keynes dominated economic thinking but their failure to recognize that full employment was an economic zone and not a specific identifiable level of economic activity found them wanting and ultimately tarnished their reputation in the public mind.

The failure of his disciples had disastrous consequences for the reputation of Keynes, who somehow came to be seen as ultimately responsible for stop/go economic policies, a belief fostered by the business community, none of whom had ever read *The General Theory* (itself a challenging exercise) and who, on the solid ground of total ignorance, believed Keynes to be an advocate for ongoing government intervention in the operations of a free enterprise capitalist economy.

By the 1960s a new term had begun to appear in the public arena – economic growth. In 1955, W. A. Lewis, an expert in economic development in what had formerly been European colonies, published *The Theory of Economic Growth*. Although the book itself was rather inconsequential, little more than a set of observations with a somewhat tenuous thread running through them, the concept which it introduced was an exceedingly attractive one. It was a term like innovation or productivity – redolent with positive connotations.

As the new term gained currency, full employment, while remaining a recognized objective of public policy, began to lose the dominant position it had previously enjoyed. From now on, full employment would be achieved indirectly as a consequence of robust economic growth.

While in itself an attractive proposition, no-one was able to go on and demonstrate precisely how robust economic growth would achieve a result which had eluded the western world for the previous three centuries.

In this process of moving the goal posts, the prospect of Utopia for the average wage and salary earner – equality of bargaining power in the labour market – slipped off the public radar.

CHAPTER 6

The rise of Neo-Smithism

As support for Keynesian policies faded in the face of the frustrating sequence of stop/go economic adjustments, public interest returned to the simple world of Adam Smith, where market forces – the interaction of demand, supply and prices – seemed able to manage economic affairs without any need for government intervention. The macroeconomic world of John Maynard Keynes began to give way to the microeconomic world of Adam Smith.

The trend was accelerated by a political accident: the emergence onto the political stage of two strong-willed economic illiterates, Margaret Thatcher in Great Britain and Ronald Reagan in the United States.

Both these individuals were enamoured of the apparently self-regulating nature of microeconomics while, like Adam Smith, being unable to comprehend the existence of the parallel world of macroeconomics. This allowed them on the one hand to endorse enthusiastically the free market philosophy of Adam Smith while on the other hand presiding over economies riddled with monopoly and oligopoly, which were the antithesis of free market activity and against which Adam Smith had fulminated. How Thatcher and Reagan were able to bridge the chasm between what they preached and what they practiced or, at the very least, condoned is a question for psychologists rather than economists.

In any case they were not alone in this ability to square the circle. The multitude of their disciples and supporters were clearly able to do the same.

From time to time observers from the left of the political spectrum sought to draw attention to the inconsistency inherent in the Thatcher/Reagan approach to economics, but for the most part they found themselves voices crying in the wilderness. By the 1980s, Neo-Smithism – the simplistic acceptance of the virtues of the free market – had become a central feature of conventional economic wisdom.

Some ten years after Neo-Smithism had established itself in the centre of public debate, the Soviet Union suddenly collapsed and with it the economic command system which it had employed since the 1930s. The proximate cause of the collapse was a foiled coup against the Soviet leader, Mikhail Gorbachev.

By then it had become increasingly obvious to the average Soviet citizen that while its government could match the United States in terms of military capacity, it was dismally failing to match the United States' ability to provide its citizens with an ever-increasing abundance of consumer goods and services. The introduction of 'perestroika' by Gorbachev had been an effort by the superseded leader to open up the now moribund economic command system wherein it was said 'the workers pretended to work and the government pretended to pay them'.

At the same time as the Soviet economic system was collapsing, the Chinese communist party was reintroducing free enterprise at the grass roots level, and doing so much to the appreciation of the average Chinese citizen and to the benefit of the Chinese economy as a whole. The 'Great Leap Forward' promised by earlier communist leaders now began to seem an immediate reality.

While events in Russian and China moved in very different directions they each contributed to a growing mood of triumphalism among the more enthusiastic Neo-Smithites. Capitalizing on this mood, business interests and their political representatives redoubled their efforts to abolish or water down existing restraints on their economic behaviour. In the United States, Neo-Smithites were even able to repeal legislation set up in the 1930s that had been designed to curb excessive financial speculation.

At the start of the twenty-first century, then, the triumphant Neo-Smithites were occupying the commanding heights of the economy. At the same time, however, many of the denizens of the plains below were less than enthusiastic about this apparent triumph of free enterprise, in particular the unemployed, the underemployed and those apprehensive of becoming unemployed. To the disinterested observer, it seemed that while economic growth was continuing to raise living standards for the population as a whole, it was still unable to ensure jobs for all those willing and able to work. There was still an unwelcome gentleman firmly ensconced on the nursery stairs, just as his predecessors had been throughout the past two centuries.

CHAPTER 7

The Global Financial Crisis

Much has been written about the Global Financial Crisis since its onset in September–October 2008. Its aftermath still dominates public policy and community thinking. As to its origins, while there is plenty of blame to go round, the primary responsibility must be borne by the then prevailing Neo-Smithite philosophy.

In 1999 the United States congress with the support of President Clinton repealed the Glass–Steagal Act. This Act, introduced by the Roosevelt administration in 1933, was designed to curb the financial speculation which had preceded and given rise to the 1929 stock market crash. The repeal of the Glass–Steagal Act represented a major triumph for Neo-Smithite philosophy because it allowed United States banks to re-enter the high-risk, high-yield areas of mortgage lending, especially in the lower end of the housing market.

Coincidentally, a new class of high-risk borrowers was emerging – individuals with little or nothing in the way of security, being encouraged to undertake mortgages both by the United States government in an endeavour to expand the level of home ownership and by the commercial lenders, prepared to lower eligibility standards in the search for extra business. Describing such groups as subprime mortgage holders helped to disguise the reality that they were in fact ultra-high-risk mortgagees. Then, by ignoring the old adage that a chain is only as strong as its weakest link, the banks were able to persuade themselves and the rest of the financial world both in the United States and overseas that they had produced a financial innovation which succeeded in maintaining high yield while lowering risk. They were then able to sell on such securitized packages or tranches to other banks and financial institutions throughout the developed world. These tranches then became the basis for further leverage or borrowings by their new owners, and the general public was introduced to new terminology – derivatives, credit default swaps, investment grade credit ratings, etc.

The first banks to go were those most dependent on short-term funding, one in France and another in Britain, followed by a major United States bank which had to call on the Federal Reserve Board for support. The two government-sponsored mortgage underwriters – the Federal National Mortgage Association (Fannie Mae) and the Federal Home Loan Mortgage Corporation (Freddie Mac) were taken into conservatorship, or public ownership, on 7 September 2008 after their share price collapsed. Later in the same month, however, the Federal Reserve Board in one last spasm of Neo-Smithism refused to bail out one of the oldest and most famous investment banks in Wall Street, Lehman Brothers, which then declared itself bankrupt with debts amounting to some US$600 billion. The result was catastrophic. Investor confidence, already shaky, turned into panic, share prices collapsed, and doomsayers began to compare the situation with October 1929 and forecast a return to the Great Depression of the 1930s.

In the months following the collapse of Lehman Brothers, Neo-Smithite philosophy was swamped by a tidal wave of dread sweeping through the developed world. Had the good times finished? Was the world economy going over a cliff? Suddenly government intervention in economic affairs was no longer a problem and, if not necessarily a long-term solution, was certainly seen as the immediate remedy.

Governments in turn responded with a variety of ad hoc emergency measures wherein principle was often sacrificed to expediency. Such measures included bank bail-outs (effectively rewarding the major culprits for their sins), money printing (rebranded as Quantitative

Easing), and a range of stimulus measures, many of them along the lines Keynes might have recommended.

Although completely unco-ordinated, the various responses of individual governments and international financial organizations had a stabilizing effect on the world economy. It might have gone over a cliff but it still managed to land on an accommodating ledge halfway down. The Great Depression had been avoided, although for most developed economies it had been replaced by the Great Recession, wherein economies are operating at sub-optimal levels experiencing inadequate rates of economic growth and undesirably high levels of unemployment. And as at the second decade of the twenty-first century, the economic prospects for most westernised economies would seem to be encapsulated by an assessment made by Keynes in 1936: 'It is an outstanding characteristic of the economic system in which we live that ... it seems capable of remaining in a chronic condition of sub-normal activity for a considerable period without any marked tendency either towards recovery or towards complete collapse.'[7]

---

7   John Maynard Keynes, *The General Theory of Employment, Interest and Money*, p. 249.

CHAPTER 8

The rich get richer

For most of the general public the Global Financial Crisis has come and gone and life continues much as it did before.

For the minority who take more than a passing interest in national affairs, the ongoing economic debate offers a choice between two quite different philosophies – Neo-Smithism and Keynesianism.

The advocates of both philosophies are pursuing the same objectives – increased economic growth and reduced unemployment – but are advocating radically different proposals for achieving them. In the nature of things much time and energy is spent by both groups in attacking the policies being advanced by the other. There is in fact much scope for such activity, given that for both groups their respective proposals each involve a reality gap.

For Neo-Smithites their reality gap arises from a failure to distinguish correctly between microeconomics and macroeconomics. In the microeconomic world of Adam Smith, surplus labour can always go elsewhere into some other area, industry and occupation. In the macroeconomic world of John Maynard Keynes, where the national economy is viewed holistically as an independent identity, surplus labour simply has nowhere else to go. The unemployed can only survive by begging, borrowing or stealing or, in the present day and age, by subsisting on some form of economic subsidy from the government and ultimately becoming part of an economic underclass of long-term unemployed.

For modern-day Keynesians the reality gap is more straightforward. The Keynesian explanation for chronic unemployment is as valid today as it was when first enunciated by Keynes in 1936. Since then, however, the economic environment has changed so radically that the solution advanced by Keynes – borrowing by the government against the expectation of future growth – is no longer a viable one.

Governments and individuals alike are already 'borrowed out' and indeed, interest payments for past loans are now operating to reduce national consumption expenditure and thus acting as a drag on economic growth.

Neo-Smithite policy and its unforeseen consequences

In line with their conviction that the best government policy is always the least government policy, Neo-Smithites see full recovery from the Global Financial Crisis as being achieved through a combination of increased investment by business and increased spending by consumers. This should be done not by direct government expenditure but by establishing and maintaining economic policies designed to encourage such behaviour. This in turn involves keeping interest rates low and by printing money – although the latter process has been rebranded and sanitized by referring to it as Quantitative Easing.

Thus far, however, both business and consumers are failing to respond sufficiently, behaving rather like obstinate horses which, having been led to water, are now refusing to drink. Both groups in their own way have a somewhat different perspective on the current economic environment to that deemed appropriate by Neo-Smithite policy. Both groups are exhibiting a substantial degree of financial caution. The philosophy of spend now and pay later seems to have lost some of its former attraction, partly because both governments and consumers are already paying later by way of interest charges on previous years of 'paying later'.

As a consequence of this waning of 'animal spirits' on the part of both consumers and business interests, the current economic scene is characterized by the historically unusual picture of eager lenders – banks and other financial institutions – far exceeding the number of would-be borrowers.

In such a situation the real beneficiaries are those individuals in the upper echelons of the income hierarchy who already possess liquid assets (as distinct from those like home owners and home buyers who only possess illiquid ones). This affluent group have been able to extend their activities in the always satisfying pursuit of asset maximizing. While investing in the stock market and in government bonds and private mortgages, they are also able to borrow additional funds on very favourable terms, as and when they feel the need to do so.

Thus a completely unforeseen consequence of Neo-Smithite policy post the GFC is that the most affluent sections of the community – the asset maximizers – seem to have been the ones who have benefited the most.

As for the rest of the community, the poor do not seem to be getting noticeably less poor, while the great majority in the middle are, for the most part, just treading water.

As matters stand in the second decade of the twenty-first century then, there seems to be no reason why this situation of the rich steadily becoming richer should not continue indefinitely.

Keynes in the 21st century

For Adam Smith, operating at the microeconomic level and thinking in terms of individual areas, industries and occupations, establishing and maintaining economic equilibrium was a quite straightforward affair. The government should take responsibility for external and internal security and for the provision of a limited number of highly desirable, but not necessarily profitable, community facilities such as education and roads. Thereafter it should stand aside and allow market forces – the interaction of demand, supply and price – to operate as freely as possible relying on the invisible hand of enlightened self-interest to ensure a steady increase in the wealth of the nation.

In complete contrast to Adam Smith, Keynes thought in macroeconomic terms, viewing the economy as an independent entity within which a multitude of transactions were continually taking place between different individuals and between those individuals and various organizations. Establishing and maintaining equilibrium in such a situation was a much more uncertain affair. Everything depended on whether at any particular time the total demand for goods and services happened to equal the total volume of goods and services on offer.

The total volume of goods and services on offer depends on a number of factors – in particular, the size of the population, the degree of skill of the available workforce, the volume of capital equipment at its disposal and the volume of natural resources available to them.

The total demand for available goods and services depends on only two factors – consumption expenditure and investment expenditure.

Consumption expenditure is a relatively stable component of total demand. For most of the population their propensity to consume is at or near 100 per cent; that is, they spend their income as or when it becomes available to them. Investment expenditure on the other hand is a 'loose cannon', erratic and unpredictable, ultimately dependent on a multitude of unco-ordinated decisions by individual business men and investors. This instability in investment expenditure makes total demand unstable which in turn tends to render the whole economy unstable.

Here then lies the essential distinction between Adam Smith and John Maynard Keynes. For Smith, viewing affairs from the microeconomic level, the situation was inherently stable. For Keynes, viewing affairs on the macroeconomic level, the situation was inherently unstable.

For this gloomy diagnosis, completely at odds with the then current conventional wisdom, Keynes proffered two separate responses, both requiring some degree of government intervention: first, supplementing private investment with some form of public investment, preferably by way of expanding the economic or social infrastructure; and second, by maintaining and expanding the stable component of Aggregate Demand – consumption expenditure – whenever and wherever possible.

In 1936 increased government investment in public infrastructure could be readily sustained by borrowing against future revenue in the expectation that the expansion in economic activity arising from the additional spending would in turn generate an increase in government revenue sufficient to redeem the original debt. Unfortunately for Keynes, or more accurately for his reputation, the economic environment of the developed world has changed radically since he first published *The General Theory*.

In 1936 'western' society was still based on the principle of cash and carry, of save now and spend later. Fewer than three generations later, the basic philosophy of all developed societies had become one of spend now and pay later. Of course even in 1936, the incurring of debt and subsequent payment of interest thereon was a very common activity. Business enterprises did it all the time by way of bank overdrafts. Individuals did it when they took out mortgages on the freehold of the property in which they lived.

But with the universal adoption of private credit cards in the decades following the end of World War II, debt has become an accepted feature of daily living particularly for those in the bottom half of the income hierarchy. The debt acceptance attitude of its citizens has spread to the governments of most democratic societies where, under the influence of populist politicians, largesse is continually being distributed to the voting population without a full reckoning of the costs to them and their descendants. Such costs primarily arise from the mandating of a portion of future revenue to meet the higher interest payments. In fact these policies can involve mortgaging the future not once but twice, since the initial outlays are justified not only on the basis of the expected revenue but also from the expected future growth.

It is impossible to believe that Keynes would have endorsed such irresponsible government policy. Brought up in a cultural environment of 'pay as you go', he would have reached the conclusion that any shortfall of current revenue below current expenditure should normally be made up by an income transfer from those living today rather than from those living in the future.

As to which section of the community should be chosen to perform such a public-spirited duty, Keynes' view can be deduced from the first paragraph of the last chapter of *The General Theory*, p. 372: 'The outstanding faults of the economic society in which we live are its failure to provide full employment *and its arbitrary and inequitable distribution of wealth and incomes*'.

Here Keynes is making a moral judgement, not an economic one. But had he been called upon to justify higher taxation for those on higher incomes, he could have done so by way of the concept which he himself introduced into the economic lexicon – the propensity to consume.

The propensity to consume measures the extent to which individuals spend their income as and when it becomes available or withhold it for some alternative use later. It is in this context that any income transfer between individuals and their government should be assessed. For those in the lower ranges of the income hierarchy any increase in taxes will lower their available income, reduce their consumption and thus act as a drag on overall economic growth. For those in the upper levels of the income hierarchy, who will have already determined in advance what goods and services they will purchase, any increase in taxes will have only a minor impact on their consumption and thus little in the way of adverse consequences for economic growth. For the individuals in this group the major impact would be to reduce somewhat the funds available to them to engage in the highly satisfying activity of asset maximizing.

Applying Keynesian analysis as enunciated in 1936 to the economic environment prevailing in the developed world in the second decade of the twenty-first century, it can only be concluded that the contribution of the upper echelons of the income hierarchy to economic growth is suboptimal.

As a group comprised mainly of asset maximizers they make only a minor contribution to consumption expenditure since their marginal propensity to consume is at or near zero. At the same time, any contribution which their activities make to investment expenditure is largely coincidental, limited to those instances where the provision of 'venture capital' is seen as contributing to the overall objective of maximizing their financial assets. Even in those situations, however, their contribution, while highly desirable, is no longer essential. There is now a surplus of liquid funds circulating through the developed economies of the world, courtesy of years of quantitative easing. Eager lenders now exceed would-be borrowers and any individual or corporation which can offer a promising business model will never be short of lenders willing to accommodate them.

As individuals, those in the upper echelons of the income hierarchy are behaving in a completely legitimate fashion. They are simply seeking to optimize their economic circumstances, as any intelligent individual should do, regardless of their place in the income hierarchy. Considered as a group, however, these individuals exert a negative impact on economic growth and unemployment.

CHAPTER 9

Inequalities within the labour force

To paraphrase George Orwell, all people are employable but some people are more employable than others. The labour force of any modern exchange economy is extremely diverse ranging from highly employable persons such as airline pilots, brain surgeons and sporting celebrities to unskilled or semi-skilled persons such as garbage collectors, gardeners and shop assistants. Occupational diversity within the labour force, although it has always been taken for granted, has quite fundamental consequences both moral and economic.

The moral consequences of workforce diversity follow from the inequality of economic opportunities available to different individuals and groups. Airline pilots may downgrade to gardeners should circumstances warrant it, but gardeners cannot take the opposite path. Some occupational inequalities translate into inequalities of income comparable with if not equal to those prevailing across the community at large.

The economic consequences of workforce diversity are more complex. They follow from the inverse correlation between individuals' employability and their risk of unemployment; the lower the former, the greater the latter. At any given level of economic activity, those at the bottom of the employability range must endure some level of chronic or intermittent joblessness characteristic of any buyer's market for labour, while those at the top of the range can usually enjoy a strong continuing demand for their services – a situation of full or near-full employment. Should the level of economic activity increase for whatever reason, unemployment will certainly diminish for those at the bottom of the hierarchy, but at the top near full employment can move to overfull employment and lead to the emergence of inflationary wage cost pressures which Keynes foresaw as a possibility in 1936 and which became a certainty in the decades following the end of World War II.

Diversity in labour force employability severely restricts any government's room to manoeuvre. In fact they can find themselves in a position akin to gridlock. Efforts to lower unemployment among the least employable workers – the unskilled, semi-skilled and the newly qualified but inexperienced – will also generate an increased demand for the highly employable workers leading to the emergence of inflationary wage cost pressures in that sector of the economy.

For the premium workforce full employment is always a possibility but for the economy as a whole, full employment is an unrealistic if not indeed meaningless concept for there is no specific level of economic activity which could ever be identified as 'full employment'. Rather there is an economic zone bounded by moderate unemployment for those at the bottom of the hierarchy and incipient wage cost inflation for those at the top. While the limits of such an economic zone can be conceptualized, they cannot, be statistically identified.

For clarity of analysis, it was proposed in Chapter 5 that such an economic zone be classified as optimum employment. The logical objective of government economic policy should thus appear to be that of narrowing the present gap between optimum employment and 'full employment,' implicitly defined in *The General Theory* in terms of a specifically identifiable level of economic activity.

Narrowing the gap between optimum employment and Keynesian 'full employment' involves narrowing the gaps in employability within the existing workforce. This in turn requires that attention should be concentrated on the development of employment opportunities specifically targeted at those in the lower end of the employment hierarchy.

CHAPTER 10

Policy options

Once the world is viewed through the lens of Keynesian macroeconomics rather than that provided by the microeconomic perspectives of Adam Smith, a range of new options emerge. Most of these options reflect, directly or indirectly, the analysis and insights offered by Keynes in *The General Theory* or in his many other writings. They would include:

1. Resurrecting economic philosophy

2. Working to live rather than living to work

3. Restructuring the taxation system

4. Work spreading

The above list is illustrative rather than definitive. It in no way pre-empts or precludes other options which might arise from independent analysis of the text contained in the first nine chapters of this work.

1. Resurrecting economic philosophy

According to his biographer, Robert Skidelsky, Keynes considered himself to be a social philosopher rather than an economist. Ironically, it now turns out that he, along with his Austrian-born contemporary Joseph Schumpeter, became one of the last economic philosophers to inhabit the planet. With the death of Schumpeter in 1950 the economic philosopher became an extinct species.

The responsibility for this untoward development can be attributed to one of the younger contemporaries of Keynes, Lionel Robbins, who in 1933 published *An Essay on the Nature and Significance of Economic Science*. This book was a powerfully argued polemic against the view held at the time by some economists and many members of the general public that economists could and should always be aware of the social consequences of any policies they might be proposing or supporting. Robbins, on the contrary, asserted that the appropriate role for economists was not to consider the objectives of economic activity, but to take those objectives as given and to restrict themselves to considering how such objectives might best be achieved.

Who then should concern themselves with what were the appropriate economic objectives for the community? Apart from a single fleeting footnote in one of the later chapters of the book this was a question which Robbins left in abeyance.

With the end of World War II and the return to peacetime conditions, western governments began to introduce new policies designed to establish and maintain full employment. It soon became obvious however that such policies had an unforeseen consequence – inflation: a continuing rise in the prices of all those goods and services used by the community.

Understandably, economists turned their attention towards this new, and distinctly unwelcome, development. If only by default, any questions relating to economic philosophy faded into the background. By 1976, three decades after the death of Keynes, with the post-Keynesian dilemma still unresolved, the area of economics which should have been occupied by economic philosophy had become something of an intellectual desert, if not indeed an intellectual vacuum, and has remained so down to the present day.

In the simple, straightforward world of microeconomics the absence of economic philosophy is of no great practical consequence. For Adam Smith and his disciples the object of economic activity was obvious: to encourage a continuing increase in the output of the goods and services and thereby raising the living standard, of the whole community.

For microeconomists in the twenty-first century the objective remains the same, although the language has changed somewhat. Economic activity should now be directed towards promoting economic growth not only for its own sake but also because of its supposed capacity to reduce longer term unemployment.

Such a simplistic objective, however, is totally inadequate for the complex economic and social environment of the macroeconomic world.

Governments and the politicians who comprise them are being continually bombarded by a cacophony of discordant voices from a vast range of diverse and usually conflicting interests. Above all else they are in need of advice from individuals and groups who have thought long and hard about what could or should be the appropriate objectives of the community's economic activity: should economic growth continue to play such a dominant role in public policy?; to what extent has the economic growth since the end of World War II actually improved the overall level of social welfare?; should the goal of increased economic growth be downgraded in favour of the Keynesian objective underlying *The General Theory*: jobs for everyone willing and able to work?

In their own self-interest, politicians, who after all are the real social engineers in any democracy, should fund the initial establishment of institutes in universities or elsewhere devoted to research and analysis of any issues directly or indirectly related to these fundamental questions.

2. Living to work or working to live

Although work, rather than leisure, has always been the dominant force in economic and social life, a number of writers, over the centuries, have argued in favour of reversing the emphasis.

The Greek philosopher Aristotle writing in the fourth century BC argued that: 'It is commonly believed that to have happiness one must have leisure. We occupy ourselves in order that we may have leisure, just as we make war for the sake of peace.'

Almost two thousand years later, the English statesman and martyr, Sir Thomas More, wrote his account of Utopia, an island in the southern hemisphere where everything was done in the best possible way. It had been visited accidently by an English sailor, one Raphael Hythloday who, having spent five years there 'returned to Europe with the express purpose of making its wise institutions known'. In Utopia, the magistrates 'saw no point in unnecessary labour, but tried to arrange matters so that the citizens are left with plenty of time in which they may develop the full liberty of the mind and the furnishing of the same. For herein they suppose the felicity of life to consist.'

Some three centuries after Sir Thomas More met his untimely end at the hands of King Henry VIII, John Stuart Mill pointed out the benefits which he considered likely to accrue from the emergence of a stationary state of economic development. Such benefits included 'A much larger body of persons than at present, not only exempt from the coarser toils but with sufficient leisure to cultivate the graces of life.'

Almost a century later, the English philosopher, Bertrand Russell, wrote an essay entitled *In Praise of Idleness* in the course of which he asserted that: 'A great deal of harm is being done in the modern world by the belief in the virtuousness of work [whereas] the road to happiness and prosperity lies in the organised diminution of work.'

A generation later, in the high noon of the post-World War II full employment boom, John Kenneth Galbraith published *The Affluent Society*. Although more a criticism of the direction economic growth was taking – private affluence amid public poverty – than of the idea of economic growth itself, the book included a chapter entitled 'Labour, Leisure and the New Class'. In the course of this chapter Galbraith argued that 'Over the span of man's history ... ordinary people have never been quite persuaded that toil is as agreeable as its alternatives. Thus to take increased wellbeing partly in the form of leisure is unquestionably rational.'

Fifteen years later, in a series of essays published under the title of *Toward a Steady-state Economy* the idea of increased leisure as an alternative to the increased output of goods and services surfaced again. In his introduction to this collection of essays, the editor, Herman E. Daly, while admitting that 'taking the benefits of technological progress mainly in the form of increased leisure was a reversal of ... historical practice' goes on to quote Bertrand Russell's essay *In Praise of Idleness* with approval as representing a policy of 'leisure growth rather than commodity growth' which will in turn provide opportunities for 'time intensive activities – friendship, care of the aged and children, meditation and reflection'.

Other contributors to the *Steady-state Economy* also emphasise the value of increased leisure. Richard England and Barry Bluestone speak of 'opportunities for the development of good interpersonal relations'. Jørgen Randers and Donella Meadows talk of the concentration of human energies on 'the development of the arts and sciences, into the enjoyment of unspoiled nature and into meaningful reactions with [one's] fellow men'.

Certainly there are no compelling moral reasons why the ordinary citizen in an affluent westernised society should prefer work to leisure. Work as an activity can hardly be judged as morally superior to leisure. On the contrary work is in fact a form of 'voluntary servitude'. For a given period of time, individuals surrender the freedom to behave in whatever way they may wish to do so and must instead accommodate themselves to the demands of others, be they supervisor, clients or customers. Nor are the activities undertaken during these periods of voluntary servitude particularly enjoyable, apart from a fortunate few. Indeed for most people work signifies varying degrees of frustration, drudgery and boredom.

Leisure on the other hand offers an immediate freedom of choice. Subject to the welfare of others an individual may engage in whatever activity he happens to find satisfying for as long a period as he pleases. He is in fact master of his own destiny.

Furthermore, from 'freedom of choice' follows the opportunity for personal self-development. Individuals have the time to develop interest and expertise in whatever area of human activity happens to appeal to them. To quote from *In Praise of Idleness* again, 'In a world where no-one is compelled to work more than four hours a day, every person possessed of scientific curiosity will be able to indulge it and every painter will be able to paint without starving.'

An even stronger moral argument for the superiority of leisure over work however is put forward by Russell in the concluding paragraph of this essay – 'Good nature is of all moral qualities, the one that the world needs most and good nature is the result of ease and security, not a life of arduous struggle.'

This apparent preference for less work and more leisure could be easily tested by any government should it ever wish to do so. All that would be required is a fairly simply readjustment of its current employment practices. Something along the following lines: first, recomputing all existing wages and salaries on an hourly basis; second, announcing the introduction of a two-tier system for the working week. The first tier would be a standard minimum period of 25 to 30 hours payable at the going hourly rate and a second optional period for which wages and hours would be determined by negotiation between the parties. The introduction of any such two-tier scheme would of course depend upon agreement by both employer and employees. If this was not forthcoming in the public sector matters would simply continue as before. The idea of a two-tier system would however have entered the public domain and any employers or employees in the private sector would be free to follow it up.

3. Restructuring the taxation system

i. The goods and services tax

Like all consumption taxes, the goods and services tax is regressive. Being uniform for all consumers its adverse impact is greatest on those at the lower end of the income range and the least on those at the upper end. These taxes were adopted in western economies during the latter part of the last century as an alternative to raising income or company taxes and have now become an accepted part of the social fabric.

As a revenue source governments of all political persuasions usually find consumption taxes invaluable. They can provide a continuing, reliable and usually substantial source of funds to finance the multitude of commitments with which governments normally saddle themselves. Left of centre political parties when in opposition can enjoy attacking publicly the unfairness of consumption taxes. On gaining office, however, such criticisms tends to lapse into default mode.

Neither Adam Smith nor John Maynard Keynes have much to say about consumption taxes. After all at the time each was writing, for neither of them was the then current structure of the taxation system a matter of public debate. However, while accepting the risks involved in trying to read the thoughts of dead men's minds, the views of both Smith and Keynes can be inferred from the ethos of their writings and from the *obiter dicta* scattered through them.

For Adam Smith taxes, while interfering with the free operation of market forces, could often be regarded as a necessary evil. After all the government must obtain funds from somewhere in order to undertake activities such as external and internal security and the provision of roads and educational facilities which private individuals motivated only by self-interest would be unwilling or unable to provide. That being so, there was little in his writings to suggest that the precise form of any tax the government might choose to impose would be of any particular interest to him. A laissez faire response to the question?!

To Keynes on the other hand an economy-wide consumption tax would have been an anathema, an unnecessary evil, objectionable on both moral and economic grounds. His moral objection is straightforward. Being regressive in its impact a consumption tax intensifies 'the arbitrary and inequitable distribution of wealth and incomes' which, in the final chapter of *The General Theory*, Keynes had identified as one of the two 'outstanding' faults of the free enterprise capitalist economy in which he lived.

His economic objection to any consumption tax was rather more complex. In the macroeconomic world the total demand for the output of goods and services produced during any given period depended on a stable component, that of consumption expenditure, and on unstable and indeterminate component, investment expenditure. Rational economic policy for any government – authoritarian or democratic – involves maintaining consumption expenditure at the highest possible level while at the same time promoting investment expenditure whenever and wherever the opportunity arises. Consumption taxes like the goods and services tax militate against the former while doing nothing to promote the latter.

The only obstacle in the way of reducing consumption taxes arises from the fact that they now represent such a substantial component of government revenue that some other source of revenue would be required to replace them.

Keynesian analysis would suggest that replacement funding for any reduction of consumption taxes could be sought from the income of those members of the community whose marginal propensity to consume was at or near zero and who, as pointed out in Chapter 8, are able to engage in the agreeable, if sometimes frustrating, activity of asset maximizing. Going a step further, as a practical compensation for such a levy, a government could offer tax rebates on any income received from investments made in any approved infrastructure projects. This would have the serendipitous result not only of promoting investment expenditure generally, but of doing so in a way guaranteed to increase job opportunities.

ii.   A more progressive income tax schedule

At this stage any attempt to introduce a more progressive form of taxation would encounter vehement opposition from the more affluent and generally more powerful sections of the community. Their self-interested opposition would be supported by the general belief now embedded in economic folklore that the wealthy play a valuable role in the economy through their ability to fund the new investment essential to continuing economic growth. In the early years of the nineteenth century, as the Industrial Revolution was gathering strength and economics was emerging as a recognized intellectual discipline, this was not an unreasonable conclusion. At the time, personal wealth was mostly held in land and the buildings erected thereon. Actual liquid assets were limited and anyone prepared to lend out their savings to others undertaking what, in prospect, might have seemed quite risky ventures could legitimately be seen as performing a valuable social function. It was of course an accolade those involved readily accepted and one which they and their successors in following generations have always sedulously fostered.

Over the last two centuries however, as the financial infrastructure of western economies widened and deepened, organizations have emerged capable of garnering private savings and channelling them into various forms of investment. Writing in *The General Theory* in 1936, Keynes noted how this was already being done by banks and insurance companies. Over the half-century following the death of Keynes in 1946, banks and insurance companies were joined by superannuation organizations and private equity funds.

By the start of the new millennium adequate funds were available to finance a zero mortgage housing boom in the United States and elsewhere. Unfortunately the boom turned into a financial bubble, and when the bubble burst, a Global Financial Crisis ensued and the world suddenly faced the prospect of a return to the Great Depression of the 1930s.

In an effort to avoid such a disaster, governments and their central banks throughout the developed world adopted a range of inflationary policies, rebranded under the less pejorative name of quantitative easing.

These policies, reflecting the dominant Neo-Smithite philosophy of the day were designed to encourage business investment. But while vastly increasing the funds available to business men and investors, governments and central banks did not, and could not, determine how those funds should be used.

In the event only a minor proportion of such funds seemed to flow into activities which directly increased employment opportunities for the working age population. For the most part owners or controllers of such funds concentrated on maintaining, and if possible, increasing the returns they could obtain from employing them in whatever ways were open to them.

As a result, in the second decade of the twenty-first century the financial situation is the exact opposite of that prevailing in the early nineteenth century at the beginning of the Industrial Revolution. Then it was a situation of eager borrowers seeking out cautious lenders; now it is a matter of eager lenders seeking out cautious borrowers.

This reversal of roles has led to two unforeseen consequences. First, in a world which is now awash with a flood of investible funds, the price of those funds – interest rates – has fallen to historically low levels and there is no obvious reason why they should not remain there indefinitely. Second, bargaining power in the financial markets has tipped in favour of borrowers. Now anyone – individual, company or government – with a record of creditworthy economic behaviour can always choose between a current form of finance and a range of the alternative ones on offer. Certainly no government in any developed economy need rely on its more affluent citizens to provide the means for undertaking whatever investment proposals they may have in mind.

In such an environment, any government, were it so minded, could reintroduce progressive scales of personal income tax without any reason to fear adverse economic consequences.

4. Work spreading

The industrialisation of westernised societies over the past two and a half centuries has resulted in a major change in the actual composition of labour demand. The continuing replacement of human energy by technological processes of one form or another has steadily reduced the previous demand for unskilled and semi-skilled labour while at the same time increasing the demand for skilled and semi-skilled individuals who will introduce, operate and maintain such technological advances.

As this adjustment process has been proceeding since the beginning of the Industrial Revolution, it is hardly surprising that in the twenty-first century the great majority of those registered as long-term unemployed should be from those in the unskilled and semi-skilled sectors of the workforce. Indeed it is possible to go a step further and hypothesise that in any modern exchange economy the pool of unskilled and semi-skilled labour is greater than is needed to produce all the goods and services which it wishes to consume – a sort of Industrial Reserve Army à la Karl Marx!

Efforts to expand employment opportunities for unskilled and semi-skilled members of the workforce could be seen as attempts to reverse the tide of history. On the other hand, from a macroeconomic point of view, such policies could be seen as halting and in fact reversing the inequality within the labour force which up to now has largely been taken for granted.

Without in any way pre-empting other possible measures the following three economic policies warrant consideration:

i.   Introducing a guaranteed income option

ii.   Establishing an environment regeneration levy

iii. Repealing minimum wage regulation

The guaranteed income option. This would be available to anyone who can provide evidence of a continuing systematic search for regular full-time employment during the twelve months preceding their application. The rate for the guaranteed income option would be significantly below the current unemployment benefit, but in return anyone accepting the option would then be free to work whenever, wherever and however they wished without any further government oversight.

Essentially the objective of any guaranteed income option is to provide those who undertake the option with some degree of bargaining power in their future negotiations with any employer.

Establishing an environment regeneration levy. For many of the activities involved in the protection and regulation of the environment a major requirement is simply the application of human energy. Much of this is already undertaken on a voluntary basis by public-spirited citizens. Government agencies, while usually co-operative in spirit, are invariably limited in practice by funding restrictions. At this sticking point an as yet unrecognized opportunity for environmental activists presents itself – advocating a specific tax to supplement the activities of governmental agencies. Such an environmental regeneration levy should enjoy strong endorsement from active conservationists and expect approval with varying degrees of enthusiasm from the rest of the community. It would encounter opposition only from those who regard lower taxation as an absolute good.

<u>Repealing minimum wage regulations.</u> Establishing, and periodically raising, minimum wage rates is usually regarded as a highly desirable form of social progress. It can also induce a warm glow of satisfaction among the more affluent sections of the community who are able to enthusiastically endorse this form of support for their less fortunate fellow citizens: a warm glow in no way lessened by any awareness that spreading such largesse does not involve any direct cost for themselves.

Broad community support for establishing and increasing minimum wage rates is always reinforced by the self-interest of the oligopolies in the labour market (a.k.a. trade unions) as a platform from which to launch fresh demands on the buyers of labour (a.k.a. employers). Yet unless the laws of supply and demand are somehow suspended when it comes to the labour market, raising the price for a service must always tend to reduce the demand for it. Thus it turns out that in practice establishing or increasing minimum wage rates has the perverse effect of impacting adversely on those whom it is designed to assist, by actually reducing their employment opportunities. Nor can they follow Adam Smith's advice to unemployed workers: move elsewhere or accept lower wages. To take the latter course of action would actually be illegal.

The microeconomic response to low wages for unskilled workers is to tinker with the normal operations of market forces in a way that will satisfy public opinion. In the process it reduces the efficiency with which that system operates, without actually increasing job opportunities except perhaps for a small number of public servants whose task it is to regulate and enforce the relevant legislation.

The appropriate macroeconomic response to low wages for unskilled workers is to refrain as far as possible from interfering with the normal operation of the market forces and concentrate instead on ensuring that, in the course of economic policy decisions, account should always be taken of their possible impact on job opportunities for unskilled workers. This general approach might be supplemented by the offer of tax rebates to employers who find themselves able to restructure their operations in a way which would allow them to employ more unskilled workers.

POSTSCRIPT

In the final chapter of *The General Theory of Employment, Interest and Money,* John Maynard Keynes identified what he saw as the two 'outstanding faults' of a free enterprise system: its inability to provide jobs for everyone willing and able to work and 'its arbitrary and inequitable distribution of wealth and incomes'.[8]

More than seventy years have now passed since the death of Keynes in 1946. Since then capitalist economies have enjoyed a phenomenal increase in the volume and range of goods and services becoming available to its citizens. Yet over the same period the two 'outstanding faults' identified by Keynes have actually intensified instead of diminishing.

For this apparent paradox the economics profession has so far failed to provide a satisfactory answer. Any attempts to do so immediately lead them into the realms of economic philosophy, an intellectual discipline they are unfamiliar with and invariably tend to avoid. Yet of all the relevant professions they are surely the ones most qualified to enter this field.

---

8   John Maynard Keynes, *The General Theory of Employment, Interest and Money,* p. 372

Seen in this context, the community in general and the politicians in particular would seem to be justified in accusing economists of shirking their professional responsibilities.

Unlike the rest of the community, however, politicians are actually in a position to remedy this situation and to do so at little or no cost to themselves or the taxpayer. This they might do by simply arranging to fund the initial establishment of institutes in universities or elsewhere, charged with the task of examining and analysing all those issues embraced within the field of economic philosophy.

Given such a scenario, the present intellectual vacuum would soon be reoccupied by a continuing flow of disinterested expert assessments across the whole of range of controversial issues which any vibrant democratic society will inevitably encounter.